BIG WORDS FOR LITTLE PE

Helen Mortimer & Cristina Tra

Being Healthy

OXFORD
UNIVERSITY PRESS

Getting ready

Every day we wash and brush to keep our skin, teeth, hair and nails clean.

Minty!

These routines are part
of our personal hygiene.

Energy

Wholesome foods and plenty to drink are important to give us the energy and goodness we need to grow and stay well.

Exercise

Our bones and muscles are made for moving in all sorts of different ways!

All different

Some of us may have a disability and do things differently.

But being healthy means the same for us all
– staying well and enjoying ourselves.

Boost

It is not just our bodies that need to be healthy.

There are things we can do to boost our mood and help us feel happy inside.

Sunshine

Sunshine is good for us and bright days make us smile but we should take care in the sun.

Allergies

Some of us may have allergies.

It is important to know about allergies
and how to cope with them.

Stay safe

We can stay safe by being aware of risks and dangers . . . everything from bee stings to road safety.

Treatment

Doctors, nurses and first-aiders try their best to keep us healthy. They are also there for us if we have an accident or become ill.

Strong bodies

When we look after our bodies,
our bodies look after us.

If we are fit and healthy then we can fight the bugs that could make us feel poorly.

Sleep

All animals need to rest . . .
and that includes us!

Our bodies and our brains can repair and recharge while we're asleep so that we wake up feeling perky and ready for the next day.

Being healthy

If we follow healthy habits we can lead healthy lives!

Ten ideas for getting the most from this book

1 Take your time. Sharing a book gives you a precious chance to experience something together and provides so many things to talk about.

2 This book is all about being healthy and looking after our bodies from top to toe. Have you had a healthy day today?

3 It's also a book about language. Ask each other how you would put being healthy into words.

4 The illustrations in this book capture various moments on a camping trip. We've intentionally not given the children names – so that you can choose your own and perhaps invent something about their personalities. What name would you give to the little dog?

5 Remember that being healthy includes looking after our mental health as well as our physical health.

6 Talk about what the children are doing to prepare for and enjoy their camping trip and think about what might have happened before and after each moment that's captured in this book.

7 Why not put together a family health poster. You could make a list of healthy dos and don'ts, decorate it and put it on your fridge!

8 By exploring and recognizing what it means to stay fit and well we hope this book will give children and the adults in their lives an awareness of the importance of choosing healthy options.

9 Encourage imagination – use a sheet to make an indoors 'tent' and pretend you're on a camping trip. You could even pack some healthy snacks to take on your expedition!

10 You could each choose a favourite word about being healthy from the book – it will probably be different each time you share the story!

Glossary

habits – things that we do at the same time every
   day or regularly

perky – if you feel perky, you feel cheerful and full
   of energy

personal hygiene – things that we do to keep clean
   so that we stay healthy and well

risks and dangers – things
   that, if they were to
   happen, might mean we
   get hurt

wholesome – healthy
   and good for our
   bodies